LEONARD J. ARRINGTON
MORMON HISTORY LECTURE SERIES
No. 20

HEROES, HERO WORSHIP, AND BRIGHAM YOUNG

by Ronald W. Walker

T0164458

Sponsored by

Special Collections & Archives
Merrill-Cazier Library
Utah State University
Logan, Utah

ISBN 978-1-60732-636-6 (paper)
ISBN 978-1-60732-637-3 (ebook)

Published by Merrill-Cazier Library
Distributed by Utah State University Press
Logan, UT 84322

FOREWORD

F. Ross Peterson

The establishment of a lecture series honoring a library's special collections and a donor to that collection is unique. Utah State University's Merrill-Cazier Library houses the personal and historical collection of Leonard J. Arrington, a renowned scholar of the American West. As part of Arrington's gift to the university, he requested that the university's historical collection become the focus for an annual lecture on an aspect of Mormon history. Utah State agreed to the request and in 1995 inaugurated the annual Leonard J. Arrington Mormon History Lecture.

Utah State University's Special Collections and Archives is ideally suited as the host for the lecture series. The state's land grant university began collecting records very early, and in the 1960s became a major depository for Utah and Mormon records. Leonard and his wife Grace joined the USU faculty and family in 1946, and the Arringtons and their colleagues worked to collect original diaries, journals, letters, and photographs.

Although trained as an economist at the University of North Carolina, Arrington became a Mormon historian of international repute. Working with numerous colleagues, the Twin Falls, Idaho, native produced the classic *Great Basin Kingdom: An Economic History of the Latter-day Saints* in 1958. Utilizing available collections at USU, Arrington embarked on a prolific publishing and editing career. He and his close ally, Dr. S. George Ellsworth, helped organize the Western History Association, and they created the *Western Historical Quarterly* as the scholarly voice of the WHA. While serving with Ellsworth as editor of the new journal, Arrington also helped both the Mormon History Association and the independent journal *Dialogue*.

One of Arrington's great talents was to encourage and inspire other scholars or writers. While he worked on biographies or institutional histories, he employed many young scholars as researchers. He fostered many careers as well as arranged for the publication of numerous books and articles.

In 1972, Arrington accepted appointments as the official historian of the Church of Jesus Christ of Latter-day Saints and the Lemuel Redd Chair of Western History at Brigham Young University. More and more Arrington focused on Mormon, rather than economic, historical topics. His own career flourished with the publication of *The Mormon Experience*, co-authored with Davis Bitton, and *American Moses: A Biography of Brigham Young*. He and his staff produced many research papers and position papers for the LDS Church as well. Nevertheless, tension developed over the historical process, and Arrington chose to move full time to BYU with his entire staff. The Joseph Fielding Smith Institute of History was established, and Leonard continued to mentor new scholars as well as publish biographies. He also produced a very significant two-volume study, *The History of Idaho*.

After Grace Arrington passed away, Leonard married Harriet Horne of Salt Lake City. They made the decision to deposit the vast Arrington collection of research documents, letters, files, books, and journals at Utah State University. The Leonard J. Arrington Historical Archives is part of the university's Special Collections. The Arrington Lecture Committee works with Special Collections to sponsor the annual lecture.

ABOUT THE AUTHOR

Ronald W. Walker (1940–2016), a respected writer and professional Mormon historian, served many years as a professor of history at Brigham Young University before his retirement in 2006. Walker was the author or editor of eight books and more than five dozen historical articles dealing mainly with Western, Utah, and Mormon history. The Mormon History Association has recognized his work with several citations and awards, including its best book award, which he received twice. Among his many roles in the field of Utah history, from research to writing, editing, mentoring, and formal teaching, he also served a term as president of the Mormon History Association.

Walker was a native of Missoula, Montana, was raised in the American midwest and the San Joaquin Valley in California, but ultimately, he made his home in Salt Lake City. At his passing in 2016, Walker left behind his wife, Nelani Midgley Walker, seven children, and twenty-one grandchildren.

HEROES, HERO WORSHIP, AND BRIGHAM YOUNG

Thomas Carlyle, at the height of his reputation in the middle of the 19th century, wrote several books about the "hero" in history, including *On Heroes and Hero Worship*. "A large topic indeed, an illimitable one; wide as Universal History itself," he wrote on the first page.

For, as I take it, Universal History, the history of what has accomplished in this world, is at bottom the History of Great Men who have worked here. They were the leaders of men, these great ones; the modelers, patterns, and in a wide sense creators, of whatsoever the general mass of men contrived to do or to attain; all things that we see standing accomplished in the world are properly the outer material result, the practical realisation and embodiment of Thoughts that dwelt in the Great Men sent into the world: the soul of the whole world's history, it may justly be considered, were the history of these.[1]

Carlyle compiled a list of hero figures, and at first glance they are an unusual collection: Burns, Cromwell, Dante, Frederick II of Prussia, Dr. Johnson, Luther, Mohammad, Napoleon, Odin, Shakespeare, and Rousseau. And there was another figure that Carlyle refused to name, although it was certainly Jesus. "Let sacred silence mediate that sacred matter; you will find it the ultimate perfection of a principle extant throughout man's whole history on earth."[2]

Carlyle had lost his religious faith while studying at the University of Edinburgh, and it has been argued that his work on the hero in history was an attempt to reclaim it in a new configuration.[3] Certainly in describing his heroes, Carlyle often employed religious images, or at least reverential ones. A true hero, Carlyle said, was a "living light-fountain," who was "pleasant to be near," and who, as "God's creation" was in "communion with Nature and the truth of things." The hero was "open to the Divine Significance of Life." Carlyle believed the hero might come from life's regular ranks and likely would be self-trained. After achieving distinction, the hero remained "simple and austere," full of purpose, sincere and assured, even combative.[4] Carlyle's hero is "an exceptional man, so different in degree from the rest of us that he seems almost different in type," wrote Ian Ousby. "His distinction is expressed in public leadership, whether in religion, literature, or politics. He leaves behind him a permanent mark on history and a permanent claim on public memory."[5]

Carlyle would become an easy target for later thinkers because of his use of imprecise words and his peculiar writing style. Sidney Hook, himself drawn to the idea that great men and women helped to shape history, put Carlyle at a distant arm's length, using strong words. Carlyle's work, Hook said, was a "tract for the times" that was "full of damply explosive moral fervour, lit up here and there with a flash of insight, but contradictory, exaggerated, and impressionistic."[6] Nor has the twentieth century been helpful. Hitler, Lenin, Mao, and Stalin were examples of the evil that some larger-than-life figures could do. "These things need to be weighed when we tell the stores of heroes," warned historian Paul Johnson.[7]

Another complaint was raised by the followers of Hubert Spencer, Friedrich Hegel, Immanuel Kant, and Karl Marx, among others. As late nineteenth-century partisans insisting upon a new way of thinking, they wished to put individuals on the sidelines. Spengler's "great man" simply became the "spirit of his times" or perhaps the "soul of his culture." Thus, at the battle of Jena, Napoleon's genius was nothing more than the "world soul on horseback." As Hook described this thinking: "Before he [the great man] can remake his society, his society must make him." Great men could not make history until the times were ripe.[8]

It is this point I wish to argue. The debate over personal and impersonal forces has recently softened as each side has given ground to find some agreement in the middle (most modern historians are concerned with the balance or weight of these forces). Yet at a critical point in history, men and women may determine the outcome of history, and one example is the role played by Brigham Young, the Mormon leader, during the early months of 1858. We shall be talking about events of the so-called Utah War, when Utahns were deciding on one of the most difficult questions facing any people—whether or not they should fight a civil war. The issue was "war or peace," and all the things that come as a result.

Young's first response after learning that U.S. President James Buchanan was sending troops to Utah in the summer of 1857 was outrage. Young ordered the eastern mountain passes to be fortified. He prepared Mormon public opinion for war. He sought the Great Basin Indians as allies. "Do I expect to stand still, sit still, or lie still, and tamely let them take away my life?" he asked one congregation. "I have told you a great many times what I have to say about that. I do not profess to be so good a man as Joseph Smith was. I do not walk under . . . [the civil officers'] protection nor into their prisons, as he did. And though [government] officers should pledge me their protection, as [Illinois] Governor [Thomas] Ford pledged protection to Joseph, I would not trust them any sooner than I would a wolf with my dinner; neither do I trust in a wicked judge, nor in any evil person."[9] Young was speaking about the events that had led to the assassination of Joseph Smith, the church's founding prophet in 1844.

Yet, in the same sermon, Young spoke of Christian restraint and providence. "Let the Saints live their religion," he said, "let them have faith in God, do all the good they can to the household of faith and to everybody else, and trust in God for the result. . . . What are we to do, under these circumstances? Live our religion. Are you going to contend against the United States? No."[10]

We have a diary that helps capture the conflict of Young's emotions. After insisting that he would not submit to "a drubbing" at the hands of U.S. soldiery, he paused. As early as the summer of 1857, he considered a general retreat, "makeing every town a "mosccow" and every mountain pass a "Potters Fieldd," ere . . . [the Saints] would permit a mobb to desceccrate the Land which God has given us." He was thinking, of course, of Napoleon's defeat at the hands of the Russians, who had adopted a scorched-earth policy. Young's diary showed another reason for hesitation: "[If] I have to fight I wish to give my enemies fair warning, and then if the[y] will not take it they must abide the consequences," he wrote. "I wish to meet *all men* at the judgment Bar of God without any to fear me or [anyone to] accuse me of a wrong action."[11]

Young's thoughts about what to do reflected the uncertainty of many Christians about whether their religion permitted them to fight a war. Roland H. Bainton's classic study, *Christian Attitudes Toward War and Peace,* found that Christians in their history had wavered between pacifism and a sanction of "a holy crusade under the auspices of God" at the other. A third and probably more popular behavior lay in the middle—waging war in a "just" fight to restore justice and peace.[12] There was never unanimity among Christians, the military historian John Keegan wryly remarked, though "the ideal of martyrdom has always been as strong as that of the justified struggle and remains strong to this day."[13]

Neither martyrdom nor crusade appealed to Young, however, who had two new books of Mormon scripture to guide him. One of Smith's revelations in the Doctrine and Covenants admonished church members to forgive their tormentors at least three times before resisting. Even then, if they should "spare" their oppressors, the Latter-day Saints were promised a reward for their righteousness.[14] The Book of Mormon, which told of ancient Christians living on the American continent, had passages that praised pure pacifism.[15] Another Book of Mormon theme was the abandonment of lands and possessions instead of fighting. Still another teaching was the possibility of engaging in a defensive war led by a prophet-general, detailed in one passage after another. Accordingly, the people of God might fight to defend "their lands, and their houses, and their wives, and their children. . . .and also that they might preserve their rights and their privileges, yea, and also their liberty, that they might worship God according to their desires."[16] On one point the Book of Mormon was certain, however. When the people became aggressors to fight a war of vengeance, God left them to their destruction.[17]

Because of the mixed signals of their religious tradition, church members in the early months of 1858 were uncertain what they should do. About two thousand U.S. soldiers had taken up winter quarters at Camp Scott in the territory's northeast corner, within a week's march of Salt Lake City. The post had been built on the smouldering ruins of Fort Bridger, once Jim Bridger's post, but later taken over by the Mormons who had burned most of it when they were forced to retreat. The Mormons had to worry, too, about several hundred teamsters and camp followers – "w[h] arf rats from St. Louis and gamblers," grumbled Delana R. Eckles, Utah's new Chief Justice, who was at the civilian outpost of Ecklesville, next to Camp Scott.[18] The rabble of Ecklesville, Judge Eckles felt, had the potential to rival any that might be found in the frontier West's celebrated mining towns, if they were ever let loose on the Mormon people.

Should the Mormons fight a preventive war before the soldiers could be re-enforced and resume their march in the spring? Or should the Latter-day Saints once again abandon their homes, just as they had done in New York, Ohio, Missouri, and Illinois in their almost thirty troubled years? Young made the first of his decisions in late February. Thomas L. Kane, a friend of the Mormons, arrived in Salt Lake City with a proposal for peace. Kane, a well connected Pennsylvanian, had received the news that Latter-day Saints were close to fighting a war with some impatience, believing that his old friends—Young and church leaders—were behaving like high spirited but undisciplined school boys. Hoping to spare the lives of the soldiers and Mormons as well, Kane had gone to see President Buchanan at the Executive Mansion and secured two letters that hinted of the president's official approval for his mission to go to Utah to mediate the controversy.[19] He had sailed from New York City, crossed the Panama Isthmus, and, after landing in southern California, made his way to the Mormon headquarters by the wagon road. "I come as an ambassador from the Chief Executive of our Nation," Kane told Young and Mormon leaders. He recommended the Mormons show their good citizenship by sending provisions to the troops at Camp Scott and by promising the army a safe entry into the Mormon heartland. He was proposing a graceful Utah surrender.[20]

Kane's proposal presumed good faith on the part of the government, and Young saw none of it. In his view, the United States had removed him as Utah's governor without notice, unlawfully stopped the delivery of the U.S. mail and other commerce, and sent an army to Utah, which was breathing out a fierce anti-Mormonism. When Young had sent badly needed salt to the army as an overture for peace, it had been summarily turned down. "What more could I have done," Young asked?[21]

Young and Kane continued their talks for the next ten days. At the top of Kane's list was the idea that Young should issue a formal proclamation urging the Latter-day Saints not to resist the army, and Kane prepared such a document for Young's signature. Young's best counteroffer was a possible letter authorizing Kane to negotiate with the army on his behalf.[22] When speaking to the Saints at their Sunday worship meeting on February 28, Young was studiously opaque. The real business of Kane was unknown to the people as well as to himself, Young said. "As for it being of much interest to you or to me is a matter that time must determine. At the present I can say it is of no moment to me."[23] Young was trying not to raise any false expectation. Writing to a church leader, Young reported that the people were trying to avoid excitement, giving themselves over to "plowing, sowing, setting out trees, &c., and also in making wise preparations for such future contingencies as may arise." There was an interesting codicil: "With us[,]" he said, "it is the kingdom of God or nothing."[24]

Young visited Kane the night before Kane was scheduled to go to Camp Scott to continue his peace mission. Young wished his friend Godspeed "with an effusion that was deeply touching," Kane recalled.[25] The smiles and embraces were gone the next morning, however. A hard-riding express rider had arrived during the night with the news that the Mormon outpost on the Salmon River, almost four hundred miles north, had been attacked by Indians and white men. Several Mormons had been killed, and Young suspected the attack had Camp Scott complicity. He was grim-faced, curt, and angry.

Kane was about forty-five miles beyond Salt Lake City, going up Weber Canyon with an escort of about a dozen Mormon scouts, when two express riders galloped into his camp with a message. It announced a change in policy. Young, as a peace gesture, had decided to offer the soldiers fifteen thousand to twenty thousand pounds of flour and two hundred head of cattle and wanted only one thing in return. He asked that Colonel Albert Sidney Johnston, the commander at Camp Scott, indicate whether he was willing to accept these provisions, which were meant to open negotiations.[26] Young never satisfactorily explained the reason for his new policy, whether he felt the attack at Salmon River was narrowing his options or whether he wanted to give peace a new try, perhaps both.

Young did not wait for Johnston's reply before taking action. "You are respectfully requested to attend and take a part with a Council of Officers of the Legion, at the Historian's Office on Thursday the 18th inst. at 2:00 pm," wrote James Ferguson, adjutant general, to the commanders of the Mormon military.[27] When the meeting convened, at least thirty men crowded into the office, across the street from Young's recently built Beehive House. In the group were three members of the First Presidency and eight apostles. It was a council of war.[28]

Hosea Stout left the best account. The object of the meeting, Stout said, was to consider "the best plan of operations to be adopted to counteract the purposes of our enemies, whether to attack them before they come near us or wait until they come near, or whether it is yet best to fight at all only in unavoidable self defense or . . . whether to fight or burn our houses & destroy everything in and around us and flee to the mountains and deserts."[29] Young was in favor of abandoning the Mormon settlements and taking his people into the desert of southern Nevada. Such a policy might let the wicked destroy themselves, just as Mormon scripture said. While Stout said that the council made no decision, Young usually had the last word in pioneer Utah.[30]

Three days later, Young assumed the pulpit to make an extraordinary address. "Should I take a course to waste life?" he asked. "We are in duty bound to preserve life," he replied, and he was unwilling to "lose one good elder." Previously, he admitted to preparing to "use up our enemies" and that many Saints were still "over-anxious" for a showdown. After considering the stakes, however, Young had concluded that a fight might bring a terrible retribution by Americans, anxious for the nation's honor. The best course, he argued, was to begin a wholesale evacuation of Utah's northern settlements, including Salt Lake City. Young acknowledged that many important details were yet to be worked out, but he was thinking of a staged withdrawal, five hundred citizens going first. Young spoke about present-day southern Nevada as a new homeland, because its lack of water might make a large army hesitant to follow. He had been thinking about such a destination for the past half dozen years, since the troubles with federal officers first began, and he had sent out explorers during recent months to find possible places for refuge. "I am your leader, Latter Day Saints, and you must follow me," Young said in one outburst. "Now we are going to see whether the sheep will follow the shepherd. I do not care whether they follow me or not."[31]

The initial reception was not enthusiastic. Only twenty-five families subscribed in one ward following Young's sermon, and the bishop of another ward complained that some were "finding fault with Pres. Young's course."[32] Margaret Judd Clawson, a Salt Lake City resident, was filled with despair. "Oh what a sacrifice after strug[g]ling to get little homes and a few little comforts around & than to leave all for a dark and uncertain future."[33] Young tried to deflect objections with humor. Citing a Biblical precedent, he said the ancient Israelites had wandered forty years to find their promised land. Perhaps the Latter-day Saints might require a little longer to find theirs.[34]

First generation Mormonism was saga, but not many episodes could match this one. Best estimates suggest more than thirty thousand men, women, and children, doing their best to obey their prophet-leader, left their homes during the spring and early summer. One early problem was snow, then came rain, which turned the single ribbon of road extending south from Salt Lake City into a thirty mile stretch of mire. Next came unspeakable dust and flies. All the skills of Young were tested to provide provisions and keep morale at reasonable levels. Most evacuees went no farther than Utah County and waited for orders. Would they be allowed to return to their homes once the crisis eased, or would they plunge farther into the unknown?

Thousands camped on the shores of Utah Lake. *Atlantic Monthly* described the situation as "a scene of squalid misery . . . a spectacle of want and distress" that Americans had never witnessed before in their history. According to the magazine's correspondent, more than half of the Mormons who had moved south "could not be accommodated in the towns," and were therefore left to find their lodging in "board-shanties, wigwams, mud-huts, log cabins, bowers of willow-branches covered with wagon sheets, and even in holes dug into the hill-sides."[35] The Mormons called the event the "Move South."

Alfred Cumming, Utah's new governor, arrived in Salt Lake City as the great evacuation was underway. He had been at Camp Scott when Kane had visited the place, and the two men agreed to oppose the spirit of military adventure that was running through the camp. Eventually it was decided that Cumming and Kane would go together to the Mormon headquarters, ahead of the soldiers and without their escort. Although Young agreed to the plan and provided men to protect them, his first reaction was to have the Mormons treat Cumming "cold enough to freeze peaches."[36] Nevertheless, protocol required that Young should pay a courtesy call, and, despite misgiving, Young went. He was accompanied by Elder George A. Smith of the Twelve. According to Smith, Cumming had a "ruddy face & grey hairs, his head was small[,] round [at] the top," perhaps with "more chops than brains." The governor was dressed in a conservative black suit.[37] Cumming had once been the image of "superb physical manhood," who walked with rapid strides and "great elasticity." But sometime during his service in the Mexican War as a sutler or more recently as a Superintendent of Indian Affairs in St. Louis, he had become a large, fleshy man who enjoyed good drink as well as food. He was well on his way to becoming a prodigious four hundred pounds.[38] He had a tendency to speak in long paragraphs, often without stopping to hear what others were saying.

Cumming fancied himself to be a superior reader of personality and, according to one secondhand report, was soon passing out assessments. Cumming thought Young was a "man of lamb-like disposition and possessed a superior brain—a mind capable of grasping everything." Smith had "an unaccountable memory [and] would make an excellent historian, and a No. 1 politician if he had a chance." Cumming gave a more mixed review to Heber C. Kimball, Young's first counselor. While "fierce, brave[,] [and] unflinching, Kimball might be more 'dreaded' than other Mormon leaders. If anyone might need hanging," it was probably him.[39]

Over the next week, Cumming and the Mormons reviewed the Utah War dispute, and more than once the talks seemed ready to collapse. Young wanted to know what instructions President Buchanan had given him, and when Cumming seemed vague on details, Young told his associates that he believed the new governor was secretly hoping for the "destruction" of the Saints and was perhaps involved in some kind of conspiracy.[40] Matters were made worse when reports reached Salt Lake City that "a white man from Johnston's camp" was offering $150 for every Mormon that the Indians killed. The Indians supposedly had been given gunpowder and lead and were promised more.[41] Some of the ammunition had been given to Tintic, a Ute leader in Utah County, who had been conducting raids on Mormon property for the past three years.[42]

Despite these difficulties, Young and Cumming slowly warmed to each other. At one point, the new governor said that he believed he might do the Mormons "a great deal of good"—if only Young would help him. The Mormons responded that if Cumming really wanted to solve the Utah question, he should go to Washington and argue the case for Utah statehood. Continuing the banter, Cumming replied that he thought that once the Mormons came to know him better, the day might come when he might serve as Utah's senator.[43]

One of Cumming's priorities was to investigate the long list of charges that former Associate Judge W. W. Drummond had made against the Latter-day Saints. After leaving the territory in late 1856, Drummond had filled the eastern press with his accusations that helped to persuade Buchanan to dispatch troops. First, Cumming examined the federal court papers that Drummond said the Mormons had supposedly burned in an act of defiance. Cumming was "astonished" to find them in good order. He likewise found the territorial library had been preserved, setting aside another of Drummond's claims. Several days later Cumming asked acting territorial secretary, William H. Hooper, to locate other territorial papers and the territorial seal – the stamping devise that validated official acts. Hooper took Cumming on an unexpected adventure. The two men climbed two high fences, walked through back lots, and finally reached a barn. There, Hooper showed Cumming the territorial safe with the missing items. Hooper explained that if the Saints actually burned the city, as Young and other Mormon leaders were threatening, Hooper wanted the government property preserved.[44] Finally, Cumming and Kane investigated the work of the former federal surveyors in Tooele. Once again Cumming came down on the side of the Mormons. He found evidence that the surveyors – bitter enemies of the Mormons – had been guilty of waste and perhaps fraud.[45]

Cumming and Kane returned to Salt Lake City on April 23 and announced their plan to go to Fort Harmony in southern Utah to find out what had taken place at Mountain Meadows. Since the troops arrived at Camp Scott, rumors had circulated that a large train of immigrants – more than one hundred fifty men, women, and children – had been wiped out. The Mormons claimed the Indians were responsible, but others were saying the local settlers were the actual perpetrators.[46] Second Counselor Daniel H. Wells hurried a dispatch about Cumming's plans to Young, who was in Provo overseeing the "Move South." "The boys don't any of them feel much like going but he [Cumming] must be cared for while he remains in our midst for . . . [Cumming's death] would be entirely too responsible a concern to go down on our hands, and I felt as though it is rather risky to let him stay so long, and hope that his life is insured long enough to last him back to [the Bridger] camp."[47] Wells's words were revealing. They showed that many men and women in Utah were strongly opposed to Cumming taking office, but, also, emotions were running dangerously high in southern Utah. Wells's letter had an undertone of something else: Some Mormon leaders, like Wells, may have suspected that the settlers at Fort Harmony had been more than innocent bystanders at the Meadows.

On the same day that Wells wrote his letter, Young returned to Salt Lake City. He had left Provo before 5:00 a.m., and Wells's letter probably reached him as he was coming north.[48] While the news of Cumming's wish to investigate the Mountain Meadows affair had not been the reason for Young returning to Salt Lake City, it may explain what later took place. Within an hour after Young arrived at headquarters, he met with Cumming.[49]

For almost two weeks, the Mormons and Cumming had been talking without coming to any kind of agreement. However, on April 24, everything changed. Although the Mormons made no record of the talks, Kane, who was present, did – at least he wrote a few jotted words and phrases in the little memo book that he carried. Kane called the meeting "final & decisive," as if a turning point had been reached.[50] Young must have known that if the Mormons were found guilty of the mass killings, the result in the current climate could spell disaster for the Latter-day Saints. He had every reason to reach an agreement with Cumming in the hope of avoiding an immediate investigation. At the very least, he did not want to be accused of obstructing justice.

Young agreed to two things during the discussion. He told Cumming that he would "cooperate with utmost heartiness with C[umming] as to Court trials," probably a reference to murders that had taken place in Springville, Utah – another item on Drummond's list of complaints. But it is also possible that Young was promising to cooperate with the prosecution of any Mormon men who had done the killing at the Meadows. Young asked Cumming to keep him informed on the progress of his various investigations.

Second, Young agreed to recognize Cumming publicly. The last event would require delicacy, for it meant an end to any lingering hope among church leaders of maintaining Young as territorial governor. On this point, Young had a recommendation for Cumming. When speaking to the Saints, perhaps the new governor might observe local sensitivities by talking of the need for peace in Utah and less about Washington's federal power.

"Well, Governor," Young said at one point (Young significantly used Cumming's title), "you are our friend but you put [a] heavy load on [the] shoulders of [the] friends of the U.S." Young was suggesting that the process of peace would be hard. Judge Eckles, at Ecklesville, was continuing to throw out threats about indicting most Mormon leaders, and the army appeared willing to back up his judicial writs by serving as a military posse. And Young wanted the mail and the transcontinental commerce to be restored as soon as possible – some of his people were literally wearing rags because Colonel Johnston was enforcing an embargo. Although so much was yet to be done, still, the quiet agreement of April 24 was an earnest hope of better things that might come.[51]

Kane saw the informal agreement as a personal triumph. "For once I am and know myself to be *happy*," he wrote.[52] Unfortunately, there was another swing of Kane's wheel of fortune, perhaps within minutes of the settlement. Word reached Salt Lake City of the death of his father. Judge John K. Kane had died after experiencing a case of "pleurisy" on February 22, 1858, at the family home of Fern Rock near Philadelphia. It had taken almost two months for the news to reach Utah, another illustration of the parallel universes existing in Utah and the East because of the lack of modern communications. "Eloi, Eloi," Kane wrote in his memorandum book— "My God, my God, why hast thou forsaken me," a paraphrase of the agony of Jesus on the cross.[53]

Several hours after the agreement, Young met with a large number of church leaders in his office, and the men reviewed the news. One report reaching Salt Lake City said that Johnston thought it "strange" that people in the territory should think that he had any "hostile intentions" against them. This item brought a stiff retort from Young. "Whether the Lord intends us to whip them [the army] out or bring them to shame in some other way I do not know," he said, giving no hint of his earlier discussion with Cumming.[54] Young was keeping his own counsel, as he usually did.

Young with his careful attention to detail calculated the "Old Tabernacle could hold 2260 adults if they weighed between 120 to 175 pounds."[55] Today's services had a congregation of three thousand, and some estimates ran as high as four thousand. The First Presidency was present as well as four members of the Quorum of the Twelve—everyone was present to hear Cumming give his maiden speech in Utah. Young began with one of the familiar topics: "The indefeasible right of the Saint to obey any law of God." Kimball also briefly spoke, after which the choir sang. Then Cumming and Kane entered through the vestry and took seats on the podium. Fortunately, Mormon shorthand clerks wrote furiously, and Cumming later filed a report to Washington, which was ghostwritten by Kane. The result may have been one of the best gauges of local popular opinion during the entire war.[56]

"I feel rejoiced, my friends, at this opportunity, which has been presented of meeting you face to face," Cumming began. "I have been sent by the President of the United States, with the consent of the Senate to be the Governor of this Territory. It is a source of pleasure to me that I have the pleasure of the friendship of this gentleman [Young], . . . who has introduced me to this stand." These were his credentials – appointment and friendship – and he tried to invoke them in a mild way. He was not an orator nor an educated man, he insisted. Nor was he among the type of "miserable" office-seekers, who had afflicted Utah in the past and who, still, "are constantly prowling round the administration" in Washington for new appointments. Cumming did not mention Drummond by name, but everyone understood that Utah's former judge was one of the men he was talking about. Such men had perverted the law when they should have been "the fulfillers of it."

Yet, amid his assurances and praise for the people of Utah, Cumming did not wish to be misunderstood. He came to Utah to "enforce obedience to the laws and powers of our common country," and he believed that in pursuing this goal he would have "the aid & co-operation of the men and women that now surround me. In fact, he said, he planned to visit southern Utah "and to present myself to the people" there. He was using a soft phrase to speak of his intention to investigate Mountain Meadows. The remark passed apparently unnoticed by the congregation. Cumming made three mistakes that he possibly later regretted. He told the congregation that the soldiers had not been "sent for any aggression upon the Mormon people," but, rather, more innocently, for the purpose of protecting them from the "lawless savage." The claim was utterly unconvincing and infuriating, a suggestion that the congregation could be so easily managed. Second, Cumming spoke of his duty to let Zion's disaffected men and women leave the territory, and before concluding his remarks, he asked one of the Mormon clerks to read a formal statement that he had prepared on the subject. The statement reflected the Gentile belief that Mormon leaders were forcing people, particularly plural wives, to remain in Utah. Like many in the congregation, Young was furious. On many occasions during the crisis, he had told those wishing to leave Utah might do so, though during the "Move South" wagons and teams were at a premium.

Cumming's third mistake was to ask the people to speak their mind. The invitation turned the worship meeting into an angry town hall discussion. While the people had sat through Cumming's remarks in "profound quiet," willing to hear him out, his invitation let loose the emotions that had been simmering among Utahns since they learned of the "Utah Expedition" the previous summer. The first on his feet was the Ulsterman Gilbert Clements, a man still in his twenties who had immigrated to Utah less than four years earlier. Clement spoke for more than an hour and gave a Jacksonian political stump speech that was interrupted at least two dozen times by wild applause and cheering. One theme was persecution. "We have suffered too much in a country which disfranchised us as freeman, robbed us of our property, imbrued her hands in the blood of our best men, and banished us beyond the pale of her civilization." The congregation responded to Clements's words with "great sensation."

Clements also talked about the outsiders whom Washington had sent to Utah. Drummond was a "unhung vagabond," whose name brought more "groans" from the people. While these "mean[,] contemptible office seekers" deplored plural marriage, they "wallowed in adultery and fornications" and "trampled under foot our laws against drunkenness and gambling!" The words about outsiders invited a comparison between Cumming, also a federal appointee, with Young. "Shall we give [up] *him* who governed us for years with such happy results – who has proved himself to be no summer friend (one simultaneous "No.") who in our dark days of adversity and sorrow stood faithfully by us in every storm, who had been a co-partner with us in poverty, nakedness, and want, who has sympathised in our afflictions, and led and guided us, as a tender parent would his child? I say shall we give up such a man, and allow a mere stranger to supplant him in our affections? ("No Never, No never, from all parts of the house").... The universal feeling of this people is that Gov. Young is, and ever will be our Governor. We may have many failings as a people; but God grant that ingratitude may never be added to the list of our short comings ("applause")."

Apostle John Taylor was the next man to speak and tried to restore calm. Although Young and Taylor respected each other, their personalities were not compatible. Young seldom included him in his most private discussions, and Taylor had not taken part in any of the talks with Cumming. Still, Taylor strongly defended Young. "I do know that Govr. Young has pursued the most pacific measures that it was possible to pursue," he said. According to this version of events, the Mormons had destroyed the supplies of the army in 1857 in order to delay its advance and therefore to avoid a battle. "For as sure as God lives if they [the soldiers] had come a little farther they would have been dead men; & if it had not been for Govr. Young, as it was they would have been dead men, & your entire army, sir, would now have been sleeping the sleep of death!" During this "most exciting time," junior officers had pled for a fight. "In the name of God why won't you let us loose on those men, we will cut them off," they had said. But Taylor said that Young refused to issue the orders. Young interrupted Taylor's speech to say: "For that they would hang me."

"*Those troops* [at Bridger] *must be withdrawn before we can have any officers palmed upon us*," he thundered in peroration. The congregation, seemingly to a man (and woman), shouted back, "Hear, hear." Taylor's colleague in the Twelve, Wilford Woodruff, believed that Taylor had been "vary hard and personal" on Cumming, and Young agreed.[57] The Mormon leader asked Taylor to temper his remarks and then told him to take his seat, which Taylor reluctantly did.

Young seemed detached when he stood to end the three-hour meeting. He had been a "little mortified" by the enthusiasm and asked for the people to remain "cool," he said. And he continued to insist that he had been a peacemaker. "I have used my powers of reason, and my influence to teach the people not to do that [which] they believed to be their imperative duty," he said, suggesting that Utah had indeed possessed an eager war party in 1857–58. Finally, he called Cumming "my friend," but gave no hint of the previous day's accommodation. "With regard to our future position pertaining to this war [?], we will see what comes." The meeting had been remarkable by any measure. Although Clements and Taylor had occupied most of the time, there were other Mormon speakers, too, and Cumming rose repeatedly to defend himself as others spoke, at times being "most roundly *hissed*," "giving him to see that the quicker he was *oph* [,] the better would they [the people] be suited," wrote Hosea Stout, the Mormons' faithful diary keeper. Yet remarkably Cumming had kept his temper and took everything "in good parts." "We had quite a discussion to day," he told Stout when it was over, certain that "all would soon be understood and work well yet."[58] For one thing, Cumming had come to realize the resolve of the Mormon people. "I was fully confirmed in my opinion that this people with their extraordinary religion and customs, would gladly encounter certain death than be subjected to the mockery of a trial of a [Delana Eckes] jury, composed of the followers of a camp," Cumming wrote Washington.[59]

The evacuation continued following the meeting, and Young set the example. One of his caravans ran almost two dozen wagons in length, and by the end of April most of his family were in Provo City, where he put his wives and children in the rented homes or thrown-up shanties, one of which was one hundred fifty feet in length. Left abandoned in Salt Lake City was Young's Beehive House, in the last stages of construction but now ready, if necessary, to be burned. Cumming asked if the Move South might be stopped? Everything depended on getting the troops out of the territory, Young replied. The entire community "would rather live out their lives in the mountains than endure the oppression the Federal Government were now heaping upon them." Cumming approved Young's order that more than 800 men should guard the abandoned property in northern Utah and Salt Lake City and tend to the growing crops.[60]

Cumming and Kane left Salt Lake City during the first week of May to examine the federal Indian farm near Spanish Fork, Utah, and perhaps begin a preliminary probe into Mountain Meadows. They were surprised to encounter Young, coming north. The two governors—the old and the new—talked for a few minutes, as Cumming was anxious to get to Spanish Fork before nightfall. Cumming told Young that he planned within the next few weeks to go to Fort Bridger and, once there, intended to ask the army not to march into Salt Lake City until President Buchanan had a chance to respond to the reports he was sending to Washington. If the army refused his request and attacked the retreating Saints, Cumming told Young that he would authorize the Utah militia to resist. This remarkable statement showed how fully Cumming had come to sympathize with Mormons.[61] The new governor was "doing as near right as he knew how," Young told the people in Salt Lake City.[62] He had come to Utah "as a tiger in disposition with the intent to destroy," but had become "as much a tiger in the right way."[63]

It is here that we will end our story, although there is much more to be told – more than can be possibly recounted in one evening's presentation. Cumming and Kane cut short their stay in central Utah as news reached them that confirmed the death of Judge Kane in Philadephia. Kane for a time hoped that the news of the death of his father might be nothing more than a rumor. However, after newspaper reports verified the terrible news, he hurried to return to Philadelphia, and Cumming also cut short his trip to central Utah. In succeeding weeks, peace commissioners would arrive from Washington to grant Young and church leaders a presidential pardon for resisting the U.S. troops. Thus, the Utah War would end and with it the Mormons' celebrated "Move South." One Latter-day Saint remembered the "glorious news" when learning that Utahns might return to their homes." Women were especially grateful and "shed tears of joy."[64] They had paid a greater price because so many of their men had been away from them, enrolled in the Utah army and unable to assist them.

We began this evening by invoking Thomas Carlyle's great man (and woman) theory. Carlyle had another candidate for his pantheon that he suggested in four pages of folio left he left in his unpublished papers. The draft had many markings and cross-outs, showing that Carlyle had given the treatment some attention. *An article on the mormons?* it began. "It were well worth writing, had one heart for it. Mormonism is a gross physical form of Calvinism, gross, physical and in many ways very base," Carlyle wrote. These last words probably referred to the scandal of its polygamy, which the Latter-day Saints had announced two years before. "But in this one point [Mormonism is] incommensurably (transcendently) superior to all other forms of religion now extant. That it is believed, that it is practically acted upon from day to day & from hour to hour. . . . That is its immeasurable superiority."[65]

Carlyle ordinarily did not like anything in the United States, perhaps because of the young nation's fresh traditions and Jacksonian Democracy.

"Cotton-crops and Indian corn and dollars come to light . . . and half a world of untilled land," he said of America with a wave of the hand."[66] Yet Mormonism, which was "still a root in this feracious [sic] Earth," was compelling. For the new religion illustrated "the value of sincerity towards one's convictions" and offered "a good illustration of the mixture . . . of Despotism and Liberty," perhaps "the perfect Form of Govt. . . . which men are so universally groping after." Mormons called this system "theodemocracy," a combination of strong leadership and a people's willingness to be led.[67]

And who was the Mormons' "great hero?" For some reason, Carlyle's unpublished essay only identified him as "Joseph Smith's successor." If he knew Brigham Young's name in 1854 when he probably wrote his essay, he did not mention it. But Carlyle believed that "Joseph Smith's successor" got things done, and had more success in his efforts than even Queen Victoria, who at the time was thought to be a powerful monarch. Brigham Young and the Mormons had a "community with a power to remove nuisances, to promote cooperations, repress contradictions & superfluities and increase the general amount of wisdom."[68] In fact, Young filled many of the Carlyle's bill of particulars for the ideal hero, including an untutored background, simplicity and assurance, and, certainly, a combative strong will, which allowed him to shape the Mormon movement.

We have told this story guided by the conviction that too often it is forgotten that great men, great ideas, and great events can be the basis of history.[69] In addition, we have raised the question of contingency. What might have happened had Young not been on the historical stage in 1857–58, with his desire for a settlement? We can imagine that possible Mormon missteps could have led to a war, with its terrible results. Is it possible that if the Mormons had fought in 1858 they might have become a battle-hardened and brittle people? Or what if events had spun out of control and Judge Eckles, backed by a military *posse comitatus*, had jailed Mormons leaders and Young and others were eventually killed – these were certainly the great fears of church leaders? Such "*what if*" questions can bring "a keener appreciation of the huge difference that choices and fortuities make in the destiny of nations," columnist George Will has written.[70]

Edmund Porter Alexander, at the time a young army officer at Camp Scott (not to be confused with the commander of the Tenth Infantry with a similar name) came to believe that Young had acted unusually wisely. Alexander, who later became a Confederate general and a widely praised commentator on the military campaigns of the Civil War, thought that

Young "knew when the time to surrender had come, and he deserves a monument for knowing it and acting upon the knowledge; even though by doing so he greatly disappointed many young officers [at Camp Scott], myself among them, anxious to see active service." Alexander compared the Mormon quest for local autonomy for their special society with other lost causes of the nineteenth century—the Confederacy and Boer insurrection—and concluded that Young "was perhaps... the wisest leader of a people seeking freedom, of all his generation."[71] It was generous praise from a former enemy.

ENDNOTES

1. Thomas Carlyle, *On Heroes and Hero Worship*, (London: Ward, Lock & Bowden & Co., 1896), 1.
2. Thomas Carlyle, *On Heroes and Hero Worship*, 11.
3. "Thomas Carlyle," *Wikipedia*, entry December 29, 2014.
4. Thomas Carlyle, *On Heroes and Hero Worship*, 2, 9, 13, 44–45, 63, and 115.
5. Ian Ousby, "Carlyle, Thackeray, and Victorian Heroism," *The Yearbook of English Studies*, vol. 12, Heroes and the Heroic Special Number (1982), 157.
6. Sidney Hook, *The Hero in History: A Study in Limitation and Possibility* (London: Secker & Warburg, 1945), 18.
7. Paul Johnson, *Heroes: From Alexander the Great and Julius Caesar to Churchill and de Gaulle* (New York: HarperCollins Publishers, 2007), 48.
8. Sidney Hook, *The Hero in History: A Study in Limitation and Possibility* (London: Secker & Warburg, 1945), 47–48, 50–52, and 75.
9. Brigham Young, Remarks, August 9, 1857, *Journal of Discourses*, 5:127.
10. Brigham Young, Remarks, August 9, 1857, *Journal of Discourses*, 5:127.
11. Everett L. Cooley, ed. *Diary of Brigham Young, 1857* (Salt Lake City: Tanner Trust Fund and University of Utah Library, 1980), August 9, 11, 16, and 19, 1857, pp. 57–58, and 61–2.
12. Roland H. Bainton, *Christian Attitudes Toward War and Peace* (Nashville: Abingdon Press, 1960), 14, 28–29, 33, and 44.
13. John Keegan, *A History of Warfare* (New York: Vintage Books, 1993), 193.
14. *Doctrine and Covenants* 98:23–31.
15. Alma 24.
16. Alma 43:8–10.
17. Mormon 3:9–16.
18. D. R. Eckles to J. C. Bright, December 13, 1857, Eckles Papers, LDS Church History Library.
19. Matthew J. Grow, *"Liberty to the Downtrodden: Thomas L. Kane, Romantic Reformer* (Yale University Press, 2009), 158–65; William P. MacKinnon, *At Sword's Point, Part 1: A Documentary History of the Utah War to 1858* (Norman, Oklahoma, 2008), 405–13.
20. Wilford Woodruff Diary, February 25, 1858; John Kay to Thomas Williams, May 10, 1858, in "Foreign Correspondence," *The Latter-day Saints' Millennial Star*, 29, no. 30, (July 24, 1858), 20: 474.
21. This conversation is recorded in Kane to Buchanan, undated letter but probably April 1858, Edyth J. Romney Typescript Collection, MS 2737, CHL.
22. Thomas L. Kane to James Buchanan, undated but probably April 1858, Edyth J. Romney Typescript Collection, MS 2737, CHL.
23. Brigham Young, Sermon, February 28, 1858, Historian's Office Reports of Speeches 1845-1885, CR 100 317, box 3, folder 28, CHL.
24. Brigham Young to Asa Calkin, March 5, 1858, Young Correspondence.
25. Kane to Buchanan, undated draft, perhaps April 1858, Edyth J. Romney Typescript Collection, MS 2737, CHL.
26. Brigham Young to Thomas L. Kane, March 9, 1858, Kane Collection, BYU.
27. James Ferguson to George A. Smith Papers, MS 1322, box 5, folder 15, LDS Church History Library.
28. Historian's Office Journal, March 18, 1858, LDS Church History Library; Wilford Woodruff Journal, March 18, 1858, LDS History Library.

29. Juanita Brooks, ed. *On the Mormon Frontier: The Diary of Hosea Stout* (Salt Lake City: University of Utah Press and Utah State Historical Society, 1962) 2 vols., March 18, 1858, 1:654.

30. Manuscript History, March 18, 1858, 2:266, LDS History Library; Mormon 4:5; Doctrine and Covenants 63:33.

31. "Special Remarks and Counsel Given at Special Council," March 21, 1857, nineteen page pamphlet, no date and no place of publication, LDS Church History Library.

32. David Candland, journal, March 21, 1858, p. 34, LDS Church History Library; North Cottonwood Ward, minutes, March 28, 1858, North Cottonwood Ward Minutes 1856–1859, LDS Church History Library.

33. Margaret Gay Judd Clawson, Reminiscences [1904]–1911, MS 3712, pp.101–102, LDS Church History Library.

34. Brigham Young, discourse, April 6, 1858, General Church Minutes Collection, CR 100 318, box 3, folder 18, LDS Church History Library.

35. "The Utah Expedition: Its Causes and Consequences," *Atlantic Monthly* 3, no. 18 (April 1859): 483.

36. Brigham Young, Remarks, Church Historian Office Journal, April 11, 2014, LDS Church History Library.

37. Historian's Office Journal, April 13, 1858, LDS Church History Library.

38. Ray R. Canning and Beverly Beeton, eds. *The Genteel Gentile: Letters of Elizabeth Cumming, 1857–1858* (Salt Lake City: Tanner Trust and University of Utah Library, 1977), 101.

39. Church Historian's Journal, April 15, 1858, LDS Church History Library. The report had an extended genealogy: William Kimball told George A. Smith of his conversation with Kane, who in turn heard Cumming's comments.

40. Historian's Office Journal, April 14, 1858.

41. Historian's Office Journal, April 13, 1858, LDS Church History Library.

42. Kane Memorandum Diary, undated entry, p. 24, copy, LDS Church History Library.

43. Historian's Journal, April 20, 1858, LDS History Library.

44. Historian's Office Journal, April 19, LDS Church History Library.

45. Alfred Cumming to Lewis Cass, May 2, 1858, Kane Papers, BYU; Historian's Journal, April 21, 1858, LDS Church History Library; and Kane Memorandum Diary, April 20–22, 1858, pp. 61–73.

46. Ronald W. Walker, Richard E. Turley, Jr., and Glen M. Leonard, *Massacre at Mountain Meadows* (New York: Oxford University Press, 2008).

47. Daniel H. Wells to Brigham Young, April 24, 1858, Brigham Young Papers, LDS History Library.

48. Scott G. Kenney, ed. Wilford Woodruff Diary, April 24, 1858 (Midvale, Utah: Signature Books, 1984), 5:183.

49. Kane Memorandum Diary, April 24, 1858, 122.

50. Kane Memorandum Diary, April 24, 1858, 122.

51. Kane Memorandum Diary, April 24, 1858, 121–22, copy LDS Church History Library.

52. Kane Memorandum Diary, April 24, 1858, 121–22.

53. Kane memorandum diary, May 5, 1858, pp. 85–86.

54. Wilford Woodruff Diary, April 24, 1858.

55. Brigham Young, Sermon, April 7, 1852, General Church Minutes, LDS Church History Library.

56. Minutes of Meeting, April 25, 1858, Brigham Young Letterbooks, Vol. 4: 956ff., which is the most complete account of the meeting. Also see Church Historian's Office Journal, April 25, 1858, LDS Church History Library and Alfred Cumming to Lewis Cass, May 2, 1858, copy, Kane Collection, Brigham Young University. The following quotations are taken from these accounts.

57. Wilford Woodruff Journal, April 25, 1858, vol. 5: 183.

58. Juanita Brooks, ed. *On the Mormon Frontier: The Diary of Hosea Stout, 1844–1861* (Salt Lake City: University of Utah Press and Utah State Historical Society, 1964), April 25, 1858, 2: 657–58.

59. Alfred Cumming to Lewis Cass, May 2, 1858, Cumming Papers, Duke University.
60. Church Historian's Office Journal, April 30, 1858, LDS Church History Library; Alfred Cumming to Lewis Cass, May 2, 1858, Cumming Papers, Duke University.
61. Church Historian's Journal, May 4, 1858, LDS Church History Library.
62. Historian's Office Journal, May 9, 1858, LDS Church History Library.
63. Mary Ellen Harris Abel Kimball Journal, May 9, 1858, MS 4218 2, LDS Church History Library.
64. Heber Robert McBride, Autobiography, ca. 1890, MSS 501, folder 1, p. 21, Special Collections, Harold B. Lee Library, Brigham Young University.
65. Clyde de L. Ryals, "Thomas Carlyle on the Mormons: An Unpublished Essay," *Carlyle Studies Annual* (1995), 50–53; Thomas Carlyle, *Latter-day Pamphlets*, cited in Paul E. Kerry, "Thomas Carlyle's Draft Essay on the Mormons," *Literature and Belief* 25 (2006), 261–88.
66. Thomas Carlyle, *Latter-day Pamphlets*, cited in Paul E. Kerry, "Thomas Carlyle's Draft Essay on the Mormons," *Literature and Belief* 25 (2006), 267–8.
67. Joseph Smith Jr., untitled, *Times and Seasons* (Nauvoo, IL), 5:510 (April 15, 1844).
68. Clyde de L. Ryals, "Thomas Carlyle on the Mormons: An Unpublished Essay," *Carlyle Studies Annual* (1995), 52.
69. J. Rufus Fears, *Books that Have Made History: Books That Can Change Your Life* (Chantilly, Virginia: The Teaching Company, 2005), 1.
70. *The Collected What If: Eminent Historians Imagining What Might Have Been*, Robert Cowley, ed. (G. P. Putnam's Sons, 2001), xv.
71. E. P. Alexander, *Military Memoirs of a Confederate: A Critical Narrative* (New York, Charles Scribner's Sons, 1907), 2.